Original title: 101 STRANGE BUT TRUE FORMULA 1
FACTS

Proofreading: V&C Brothers

Writers: Víctor Martínez Cerdá and Carlos Martínez
Cerdá (V&C Brothers)

Layout and design: V&C Brothers

101
STRANGE BUT TRUE
FORMULA 1 FACTS

1

Ever wondered why F1 is known as the "Great Circus"?

It's because it's like a huge travelling family of mechanics, bosses, organisers, suppliers and logistics companies.

The same faces are seen the world over at every circuit, like a touring circus.

The name Great Circus was first used back in the 50's and recalls the famous Roman circus, bringing the fans and circuits very firmly into the F1 mix.

2

Why are F1 cars fitted with the halo?

The halo is a safety feature introduced into F1 for the 2018 season as a result of Jules Bianchi's horrific crash in the 2014 Japanese Grand Prix.

It surrounds the cockpit and protects the driver from flying parts, tyres and track debris and can withstand an impact of up to twelve tonnes: although initially unpopular because of its appearance, its effectiveness in a string of crashes and mishaps has proved its effectiveness.

3

Pirelli introduced new larger tyres in 2022, with rims being changed to eighteen inches from the previous thirteen inches.

The Italian manufacturer carried out more than ten thousand hours of testing, over five thousand hours of simulation and developed more than seventy virtual prototypes over twenty thousand track kilometres by different teams.

The increased size initially drew complaints from drivers about poor visibility, although they soon grew accustomed to the new tyre.

4

The 2005 United States Grand Prix went down in history as the greatest F1 embarrassment in living memory.

Throughout 2005, a bitter tyre war was raging between Michelin and Bridgestone.

Going into Indianapolis, the teams using the Michelin compound found that their tyres could not cope with the loads created by the oval track, exposing drivers to the risk of high speed accidents.

Before the race, Michelin lobbied to include a chicane to reduce speed and minimise the risk on the oval, but it was refused and on the next day's formation lap the teams with Michelin rubber pitted and refused to form up.

Only six cars (all on Bridgestone) raced: Ferraris, Jordans and the Minardi.

The fans began booing and throwing things onto the track in protest.

The race was Michael Schumacher's only victory in 2005 and Jordan's last podium and it left a bitter memory in the minds of American fans, which took years for F1 to overcome.

5

**Max Verstappen holds the record
for the fastest pit stop in history.**

His pit stop tyre change record is
1.82 seconds set during the
Brazilian GP in 2019, a race
that the Dutchman won.

The record is unlikely to be broken
in the near future: 2022 tyres are
heavier than before and to make
matters worse, F1 introduced
sensors midway through 2021 to
monitor the speed of the tyre
change to reduce the danger of a
bad fit.

6

**In 2014, F1 entered the hybrid era,
amid heavy criticism.**

The engines were slower and quieter, making for more boring races and there was little equality.

It was also a statistical disaster, with only Mercedes winning until 2021.

The German team's superiority inflated Lewis Hamilton's F1 results.

Back in the era of naturally-aspirated V8 engines, Hamilton lagged behind Sebastian Vettel and Fernando Alonso.

Luckily though, Ferrari and Red Bull began to challenge Mercedes again, bringing the sport back into the limelight and increasing ticket sales.

7

Pirelli's multi-coloured compounds.

The Italian tyre manufacturer designed its tyre range to display track performance. Red is the softest compound, white the hardest, with yellow sandwiched between them.

The softer a tyre is, the faster it goes off, with the reverse being true for a hard compound.

Rain tyres are distinguished by green used for intermediate conditions, and blue for heavy rain.

The latter can clear up to thirty litres of water a second at 300 km/h. Until 2018, there were also ultra-soft, hyper-soft and super-hard tyres, in other colours including pink and sky blue but F1 simplified the rule the following year to make the races easier to understand for the fans, leaving red, yellow and classic white as the standard colours.

Now there are five degrees of hardness: C1 (hardest), C2, C3, C4 and C5 (softest). At each GP, F1 uses three compounds depending on the characteristics of the track, although the colours never change.

8

**The last time we saw refuelling was
at the 2009 Brazilian GP.**

Since then, F1 has fought hard to prevent
its return for several reasons: the quest
for greater safety from fires and filler
accidents, to reduce costs and to
reduce the weight of the cars.

This is somewhat contradictory, as cars
have been getting wider over the last
decade and now F1 is going down the
road of electrification.

This has put an end to those scary scenes
from the pits of yesteryear like Jos
Verstappen's fire in Germany 1994, Eddie
Irvine's in Belgium 1995 or when Felipe
Massa lost the filler hose in the pit lane
at the 2008 Singapore GP.

9

What is DRS and how does it work?

The Drag Reduction System was introduced to F1 in the 2011 season to encourage overtaking on the straights.

The system reduces drag and is activated when the driver presses a button on the steering wheel that opens the rear wing, increasing speed.

It can only be activated in a straight and only if the chasing driver is less than a second behind his rival.

DRS has definitely made racing more exciting and has been instrumental in victories over the last decade, although many critics would prefer to see it banned as it helps create artificial overtakes.

10

In recent years, sustainability has become an important topic for Formula 1 and its teams, and they have begun to take measures to reduce their environmental impact.

In this sense, Formula 1 has set an ambitious goal of becoming fully sustainable by 2030.

One of the measures they have taken to achieve this is the introduction of E10 fuel in their race cars.

E10 fuel is a blend of gasoline and ethanol, where ethanol represents 10% of the blend.

Ethanol is a renewable biofuel produced from plant materials such as corn or sugarcane.

The aim of this fuel blend is to reduce greenhouse gas emissions produced by the race cars during races.

Some teams have reported a loss of power in their race cars due to the use of this new fuel, as gasoline is a more powerful fuel than ethanol.

However, Formula 1 is working on solutions to improve fuel efficiency and race car power, without compromising their sustainability goals.

In addition to the use of more sustainable fuels, Formula 1 is also working on other initiatives to reduce its environmental impact.

For example, they are working on the development of more efficient technologies and reducing waste and emissions during race events.

11

KERS, the Kinetic Energy Recovery System, was F1's first real taste of electrification.

It was a regenerative brake that acted just like a video game turbo, providing extra power to the drivers for just over six seconds a lap.

For each completed lap, KERS was recharged and was particularly useful in accelerating out of a corner and when overtaking.

Introduced in 2009, some teams initially rejected it because it was too heavy and made no improvement to overall performance.

Over the years, KERS became lighter and the entire grid was using it until the 2013 season, although the following year engine hybridisation would make KERS obsolete.

12

Fernando Alonso and Max Verstappen are two Formula 1 drivers who have achieved a unique feat in their careers: dethroning two different seven-time champions.

Alonso, a Spanish driver, ended the consecutive title streak of German Michael Schumacher in the 2005 season, while Verstappen, a Dutch driver, stopped the streak of British driver Lewis Hamilton in the 2021 season.

It is interesting to note that both drivers share a peculiar aspect in their careers: according to Verstappen's statements on several occasions, he used to use Alonso's car in old Formula 1 video games, as he identified with his driving style and skill on track.

It seems that this influence has been one of the keys for both drivers to overcome the seven-time champions and achieve success in Formula 1.

It is also worth noting that there was a historic hug between the two drivers.

It was an emotional moment in the 2021 season, when Alonso and Verstappen met in the paddock of the Abu Dhabi Grand Prix.

After an intense battle on the track, Verstappen clinched the world title and Alonso congratulated him with a warm hug.

This moment has become an unforgettable memory for Formula 1 fans, as it represents the greatness of two exceptional drivers who have overcome great challenges and become world champions.

13

Maria Teresa de Filippis was the great pioneer of women's motorsport.

She was the first woman to compete in F1, at a time when the nicest thing she was told was "the only helmet you can wear is the one at the hairdresser's".

The Italian entered five Grand Prix, making her debut in Monaco and finishing tenth in Belgium in 1958.

She maintained a friendship with five-time champion Juan Manuel Fangio but retired from racing the following year after the death of Jean Behra.

She drove for high-end marques like Maserati and Porsche, and inspired more women in the following decades, breaking the moulds of a male-dominated society.

She died in 2016 at the age of eighty-nine.

14

Which circuit has hosted the most F1 races?

It's not Silverstone, Spa or Monaco but the Autodromo Nazionale di Monza.

The famous temple of speed has hosted seventy-one F1 Grand Prix uninterruptedly since 1950, when the class was founded with the only break in 1980 for resurfacing when it was moved to Imola although Monza is without doubt the Tifosi's favourite, who always bring their passion for Ferrari with them.

The Italian circuit has seen some amazing victories, but the most memorable will always be those in Ferrari red: Ascari, Hill, Surtees, Scarfiotti, Regazzoni, Scheckter, Berger, Schumacher, Barrichello, Alonso and Leclerc.

15

We are used to a Grand Prix starting on Friday with free practice, Saturday with qualifying and Sunday with the race, however, Monaco is different.

Assumption Day is an important tradition in Monte Carlo and is celebrated on Thursday so in 1950, the organisers decided that practice would be held on Thursday to attract more spectators, leaving Friday as a rest day.

However, the religious custom was gradually lost and in 2022, practice was held on Friday, although Formula 2 races had already been held on Friday for several years.

16

Francisco Godia Sales, better known as Paco, made his debut in 1951 at the Pedralbes circuit in Barcelona for the Spanish Grand Prix, sharing his debut with Juan Jover, although the Barcelona-born driver was unable to start so the credit for being the first Spanish driver in the history of F1 went to Godia.

The Catalan Maserati driver returned to race at Pedralbes in 1954 and two years later, the legendary Italian marque prepared a semi-official car for him to drive for the entire season.

It was his best year, finishing fourth at the Nürburgring and Monza and scoring his first world championship points. Paco, renowned as a gentleman driver, left the Great Circus in mid-1958.

However, his contribution was major and his legacy led to the creation of the Circuit de Barcelona-Catalunya.

After Godia, a dozen Spanish drivers came to F1, the most famous of which is obviously Fernando Alonso.

17

The F1 cars of the new era starting in 2022 weigh a minimum of 795 kilos.

Over the past two decades, the cars have grown in size and weight due to new safety requirements.

Today's F1 cars are the heaviest in history.

This makes them harder to handle in the bends but this is compensated for by downforce and power steering, making them easier to corner, and capable of speeds in excess of 300 km/h on any circuit except Monaco.

18

The 1955 Hours Le Mans disaster.

Although not a F1 Grand Prix, the accident had a lasting impact on the competition.

Pierre Levegh's Mercedes 300 SLR took off on the main straight at La Sarthe, killing eighty-four people, including the French driver, and injuring around 120 when his car careered into the grandstand in a fireball.

The tragedy led to Mercedes dropping out of racing for more than three decades and several countries, including France and Spain, were reluctant to host motor racing events for some time.

The most extreme case was Switzerland, which took six decades to allow motor racing to return, and only relented with the introduction of Formula E.

19

Formula 1 drivers are subjected to great physical demands during a race and usually lose between 3 and 5 kilograms of body weight per race due to sweating and dehydration.

This weight loss is caused by several reasons, including the high temperature in the car's cockpit, the G-forces they are subjected to, and the need to maintain high concentration and precision throughout the race.

G-forces are a measure of acceleration experienced by a body relative to the Earth's gravity.

In Formula 1, cars are capable of accelerating and braking at a very high speed, causing a great amount of G-forces on the drivers.

During a race, drivers can experience up to 5 Gs in the tightest corners, which means their effective weight is multiplied by five.

This can be very taxing on the human body, and drivers must be in excellent physical shape to endure it.

In addition, the environment in the car's cockpit is extremely hot, with temperatures that can reach 50 degrees Celsius in some races.

Drivers must wear special suits that keep them cool and dry, but they can still lose a great amount of fluids through sweating.

This dehydration can be very dangerous for drivers as it can affect their concentration and ability to make precise decisions.

Overall, Formula 1 drivers must be in excellent physical shape to compete in these demanding races.

Many drivers train daily to improve their cardiovascular and muscular endurance, and follow a careful diet to ensure their body is in optimal condition to compete.

Weight loss and dehydration are just some of the side effects of competing in these races, but drivers are willing to face these challenges to achieve glory on the track.

20

The Indianapolis 500 and its relationship with F1.

The mythical 500 was an official F1 World Championship race throughout the 50's, but during the 60's it began to move away from the F1.

Many of F1's most famous drivers have won on the world's most prestigious oval: Clark, Hill, Andretti, Fittipaldi, Villeneuve, Montoya and Sato.

Fernando Alonso came close to winning the Indy 500 ring in 2017, like Álex Palou in the 105th race in 2021.

The Barcelona-born driver eventually finished second, fighting for victory until the last lap.

21

HANS, which stands for "Head and Neck Support," is a safety device used in motorsports, especially in Formula 1 and other high-performance competitions.

It is a collar that is placed around the driver's neck and is designed to prevent neck and spinal injuries in case of an impact or sudden deceleration.

HANS was developed by American doctor Robert Hubbard and his brother Jim in the 1980s.

The device consists of two pads that rest on the driver's shoulders and are secured to the helmet with straps.

These straps prevent the head from moving forward and backward in the event of an impact, thus reducing the risk of neck and spinal injuries.

Formula 1 introduced the mandatory use of HANS in 2003, following several serious accidents in which drivers suffered neck and spinal injuries.

Since then, it has been demonstrated that HANS is a very effective device for preventing high-severity injuries.

In fact, according to studies conducted by the FIA (International Automobile Federation), the use of HANS has significantly reduced the risk of head and neck injuries for drivers.

Currently, HANS is a mandatory safety device in many motorsport competitions around the world.

In addition, it has become an essential element of drivers' personal protective equipment, along with helmets, gloves, and fire-resistant suits.

The use of HANS has proven to be a major breakthrough in the safety of Formula 1 drivers and has saved many lives in serious accidents.

22

Formula 1 drivers do not have access to a bathroom during a race, and the need to urinate may arise during the race.

In these cases, drivers often choose to urinate inside their racing suit, as stopping the car to go to the bathroom is not a practical option.

Drivers' racing suits are designed to absorb and eliminate moisture, which means that urine will dry quickly and not cause too much discomfort during the race.

In addition, drivers often wear special underwear designed to absorb moisture and prevent skin irritation.

It is important to note that drivers often remain well hydrated during races, as they lose a significant amount of fluids due to heat, physical exertion, and stress.

They drink water and isotonic drinks through a tube connected to the mouth, which is called a hydration system.

This system allows them to drink while driving without the need to stop the car.

23

The "Green Hell" is what three-time champion Jackie Stewart once called the twenty-two-kilometer, famously dangerous Nordschleife circuit in the middle of a German forest.

Drivers always found the old Nürburgring a mental and physical challenge and accidents were common.

It was here that Niki Lauda almost lost his life in 1976 in what was to be the last Nordschleife F1 race.

The Grand Prix returned to the remodelled and much safer Nürburgring decades later.

24

Since the beginnings of Formula 1, the winner of a Grand Prix was crowned with a laurel wreath.

This tradition dates back to ancient Greece, where athletes were awarded in this way at the Olympic Games.

However, in 1985, Bernie Ecclestone, who was the head of F1 at the time, decided to eliminate the laurel wreath as a prize for Grand Prix winners.

The reason was that the wreath covered the sponsor's stickers, who wanted their logos to be visible in the winner's image.

Therefore, Ecclestone decided that a new way of rewarding the winners had to be found.

In 2021, the laurel wreath made a comeback in the sprint races that were introduced for that season.

The winners of the sprint races received a laurel wreath as recognition for their victory.

Although this tradition has not been reintroduced in regular Grand Prix races, many fans and drivers were glad to see the return of this historic tradition in Formula 1.

25

F1 has long banned the number thirteen.

There is no garage bearing the number and in the past, when the numbers were allocated according to the position of the constructors in the standings, the teams avoided it.

Things have never gone well for whoever used the number thirteen in F1 with two consecutive deaths in 1925 (Paul Torchy), and 1926 (Giulio Masetti).

In recent history, four drivers have tried racing as number thirteen but fires, retirements and failure to qualify reinforced the curse. Most recently, Pastor Maldonado.

The Venezuelan used the number on his Lotus during the 2014 and 2015 seasons, and retired from F1 with almost more retirements than points in those two seasons!

26

Drivers are not allowed to do doughnuts, (although it's more of a recommendation than a ban.)

Team managers are against victory doughnuts as it seriously reduces the lifetime of the engine.

Current rules state that a team can only use three engines per season.

If a fourth is required, a grid penalty is imposed so they just have to contain their excitement!

That's why the only time we see the drivers celebrating their success is at the last Grand Prix of the year, when there is no need to think about the engine for the next race.

27

How much power does an F1 car put out?

It's estimated that the 1,000 horsepower barrier has already been broken in the hybrid era.

V6 1.6 turbo engines are getting more and more powerful and even with the arrival of E10 fuel an increase is expected, despite initial doubts in 2022.

Five years ago, the claimed 1,007 horsepower of Fernando Alonso's McLaren-Honda was disputed and on track it proved to be nowhere near that figure.

Some years later, the Japanese manufacturer triumphed with Red Bull and Max Verstappen, overtaking Lewis Hamilton's all-powerful Mercedes in 2021.

28

How much does an F1 car cost?

When all the components are taken into account, the total build cost is almost ten million euros, with the single most valuable element being the engine.

This alone can cost up to four million euros.

The gearbox alone costs around 500.000, exhausts and brakes half that, and front and rear spoilers more than 100.000.

Every oil leak, every shunt, can cost a team millions, especially considering the budget limit set by the organisation.

29

The recovery of the "ground effect".

Between 1978 and 1982, F1 employed the technique on all cars.

The new structure of the bottom of the car allowed higher cornering speeds and a more efficient airflow.

However, it was dangerous and led to fatal accidents when the car bottomed out and took off because of the skirts.

In 2022, ground effect is back, albeit with redesigned skirts, but now the problem is rebound, which is unsettling for drivers going flat out.

F1 brought back ground effect to allow more overtaking with less turbulence, and so far it's working, with more exciting races and more duels on track.

30

What's the top speed ever recorded for an F1 car?

Valtteri Bottas holds this particular record.

The Finn set it in 2016, during qualifying for the Azerbaijan GP.

The Williams was on the tail of Max Verstappen's Red Bull on the circuit's two-kilometre-long straight and reached 378 km/h.

Now, with heavier cars and more drag, it is unthinkable that this could be beaten in the near future.

There is one exception though: the BAR-Honda team covered the air intakes and removed the rear wing during tests on a salt flat.

The car hit 413 km/h, although this speed was obviously not recorded in a Grand Prix and the car was set up for the attempt.

31

The Indianapolis 500 is one of the most iconic races in the world of motorsport, and for a time, it had an unusual connection with Formula 1.

History with F1: Surprisingly, the Indianapolis 500 was part of the Formula 1 World Championship from its inception in 1950 until 1960. This means that during those years, drivers who participated in the Indianapolis 500 earned points for the Formula 1 World Championship. However, it's important to note that few European F1 drivers made the trip to the United States to compete in this race, and likewise, few American drivers from the Indy 500 traveled to Europe to compete in other F1 races.

Regulatory Differences: Despite being on the F1 calendar, the Indianapolis 500 did not adhere to the same technical regulations as the rest of the F1 championship. Indy cars were different from the typical single-seaters of Formula 1, leading to a regulatory mismatch. Ultimately, due to these differences and other factors, the race was removed from the F1 calendar after 1960.

Drivers' Choices: Over the years, and especially in more recent times, there have been drivers who have shown interest in competing in the Indianapolis 500, even if it meant missing another significant race on the F1 calendar, like the Monaco Grand Prix. This was the case with Jim Clark, who won the Indy 500 in 1965, and Fernando Alonso, who chose to compete in Indianapolis in 2017 instead of Monaco, in an attempt to achieve the motorsport "Triple Crown" (Winning the Monaco Grand Prix, the Indianapolis 500, and the 24 Hours of Le Mans).

32

Both Great Britain and Italy have hosted at least one Grand Prix in every season of Formula 1 since its creation in 1950.

In fact, these two countries are the only ones that can boast of having organized an F1 race every season.

In Great Britain, most F1 races have been held at the Silverstone circuit, although they have also been held at other circuits such as Aintree, Brands Hatch, and Donington Park.

In Italy, the F1 race has mainly been held at the Monza circuit, although it has also been held at other circuits such as Imola.

It is important to note that the circuits that have hosted Grand Prix races in these countries have changed over the years.

For example, the British Grand Prix was held at Aintree from 1955 to 1962 before moving to Silverstone.

Additionally, the San Marino Grand Prix was held at the Imola circuit instead of Monza from 1981 to 2006.

33

The most powerful Formula 1 teams, such as Mercedes, Ferrari, McLaren, and Red Bull, can have a large number of people working for them.

These teams can have up to 600 people working to ensure their cars can compete and be successful on the track.

The personnel working in these teams include drivers, engineers, mechanics, designers, aerodynamics experts, logistics managers, data analysts, and others.

Additionally, these teams usually have high-tech facilities and advanced resources, allowing them to conduct extensive testing and analysis to improve the performance of their cars.

However, not all Formula 1 teams have the same economic capacity and cannot afford to have so many people working on their team.

Smaller teams have much lower budgets and therefore have fewer resources at their disposal.

Often, these teams have to be creative and find innovative ways to do more with fewer resources, which can be a challenge.

34

The Red Bull Racing team of mechanics showcased their skill and precision at the 2019 Brazilian Grand Prix.

At that event, they managed to change all four tires of Max Verstappen's race car in just 1.82 seconds, setting a new standard in F1 pit stops.

This feat not only reflected the expertise and training of the mechanics but also the meticulous planning and coordination required to execute a pit stop at such speed.

This ultra-fast pit stop was a pivotal component in Verstappen securing the victory in that race.

However, Red Bull didn't stop there.

Their commitment to excellence and continuous improvement led them to break the two-second barrier on more than one occasion.

At the 2021 Hungarian Grand Prix, they achieved a time of 1.88 seconds, and later, at the Bahrain Grand Prix, they executed a pit stop in 1.93 seconds.

These records stand as a testament to the dedication, training, and innovation that drives teams like Red Bull in their relentless pursuit of perfection in a sport where every fraction of a second counts.

It's a clear demonstration of how the combination of cutting-edge technology, human skills, and coordination can achieve feats that would seem impossible at first glance.

35

During a Formula 1 Grand Prix, the intensity and complexity of the circuit largely determine the frequency with which a driver shifts gears.

Number of Shifts: On an average circuit, it is estimated that F1 drivers make between 2,500 and 4,000 gear changes over the course of a race. This means that each lap involves numerous speed adjustments to adapt to the different characteristics of the track, such as tight corners, chicanes, and long straights.

Circuit Morphology: The structure and design of a circuit play a crucial role in the number of gear shifts a driver must make. Tracks with a mix of long straights followed by series of technical corners require more shifts to optimize speed and performance across different sections of the circuit. In contrast, a simpler layout with fewer variations might reduce the number of necessary shifts.

Indianapolis Oval: Using the Indianapolis oval as an example is illustrative. Although Formula 1 doesn't regularly race on ovals, if they were to do so at a venue like Indianapolis, the number of gear changes would drop drastically. On ovals, most of the race is conducted on straights or high-speed curves where cars can maintain a high gear for an extended period.

36

During the time a Formula 1 driver is racing on a circuit, the distance between the bottom of the car and the asphalt is very small.

In fact, it's usually around 50 millimeters, which is approximately the width of an iPhone.

This small distance is due to Formula 1 teams seeking to minimize the air resistance that the car encounters on its way, which allows them to be faster.

To achieve this, cars are often designed with a very low suspension, which makes them very close to the ground.

Additionally, the car's height can vary slightly during the race, as the suspension is designed to adapt to track conditions and the car's speed.

This small distance can also generate sparks when the car touches the asphalt in some turns or when there is a light contact with other cars.

This happens because the friction between the car's bottom and the asphalt can generate enough heat to make sparks appear.

37

On a Grand Prix Sunday, between the two cars of each team, an average of 1.200 litres of fuel is consumed.

To put that in context, it is twenty times more than the fuel consumption of a Hyundai i10, which is a highly efficient car, capable of covering the distance between Madrid and Valencia (360 kilometres) on a single tank.

That's a massive gulf by any reckoning, considering that a GP can take between an hour and a half and two hours if there are no safety cars out.

38

Formula 1 cars are capable of achieving impressive speeds in a very short amount of time.

The time it takes to accelerate from 0 to 100 km/h can vary slightly from one car to another and from one season to another, but it is usually around 2.6 seconds, as you mentioned.

But what is even more impressive is the acceleration they can achieve after reaching 100 km/h.

For example, they can go from 0 to 200 km/h in around 4.5 seconds, and from 0 to 300 km/h in about 10 seconds.

This is possible thanks to the highly sophisticated and powerful engines used by Formula 1 cars, as well as the incredible efficiency of their aerodynamics and tires.

Drivers must be very well physically prepared to withstand the G-forces they are subjected to during acceleration, especially in the first turns of the race.

39

The deceleration force that a Formula 1 driver experiences when fully braking to take a turn is really intense.

According to some studies, this force can reach up to 5G (five times the force of gravity), which means that the weight of the driver is multiplied by five at that moment.

To put it into perspective, a normal street car experiences a braking force of around 0.7G in a strong brake.

This force is so intense that Formula 1 drivers have to train specifically to be able to withstand it and stay in shape.

In fact, the neck is one of the body parts that suffers the most in this discipline, as it has to support the weight of the head while moving at high speeds and experiencing extreme deceleration forces.

That's why drivers usually do specific exercises to strengthen their neck muscles and avoid injuries.

40

The steering wheels of Formula 1 cars are extremely complex, with a large number of buttons and settings that the driver can use to optimize the car's performance.

The buttons vary from team to team and from driver to driver, as they are adapted to the individual preferences and needs of each driver.

Some of the buttons mentioned are fundamental for managing an F1 race.

For example, the button to redirect to the pit lane allows the driver to enter the pits for a stop quickly and safely.

There is also the speed limiter to enter the pit lane correctly, which helps control the car's speed while entering the pit area, where the speed is limited to 80 km/h.

The brake balance adjustment is a key tool for achieving car stability while braking, as it can adjust the amount of brake applied to each wheel.

The DRS (Drag Reduction System) is a device used in specific areas of the track where it is allowed, and it reduces the car's air resistance, allowing for increased top speed and facilitating overtaking.

In addition to these buttons, the steering wheels also have buttons to control the transmission differential, suspension adjustment, engine management, and radio activation to communicate with the team in the pits.

There are also buttons to control fuel consumption and battery charging, which are crucial in an F1 race.

All these adjustments and configurations are made in real-time while the driver is driving at incredible speeds, which requires great skill and concentration.

41

The power unit is one of the key components in a Formula 1 car and consists of several elements, including the internal combustion engine (ICE), the energy recovery system (ERS), and the electronic control unit (ECU).

The internal combustion engine is the heaviest component of the power unit, usually weighing around 145-150 kg.

This is partly due to FIA regulations that limit the use of advanced materials and technologies, forcing manufacturers to find a balance between performance and durability.

The energy recovery system (ERS) also contributes to the total weight of the power unit and consists of several components, such as the thermal motor-generator unit (MGU-H), the kinetic motor-generator unit (MGU-K), the battery, and the electronic controller.

In total, the ERS system can weigh around 30-35 kg.

The electronic control unit (ECU) is a critical component that manages the engine and ERS system's operation and can also weigh several kilograms.

In summary, the power unit of a Formula 1 car can weigh around 180-190 kg, with the internal combustion engine being the heaviest component.

42

High temperatures are a factor to consider in some Formula 1 races, especially in countries with tropical climates such as Malaysia, Singapore, or Brazil.

In these places, humidity and heat can cause the temperature inside the cockpit to exceed 50 degrees Celsius, which represents a great challenge for the drivers.

To combat the heat, drivers undergo specific training to improve their cardiovascular endurance and heat tolerance.

They also use cooling systems built into the seat and clothing that help keep their body temperature under control.

Additionally, teams make adjustments to the car's ventilation to ensure the driver receives enough fresh air during the race.

All of this is essential to avoid dehydration and exhaustion that can negatively affect the driver's performance.

43

In rainy conditions, Formula 1 teams use special soft compound tires with deep treads to evacuate water and provide traction on wet surfaces.

These wet weather tires have deeper treads than dry weather tires, and the grooves in the tread widen to evacuate water.

As for the amount of water wet tires can evacuate, as mentioned in the statement, it is said to be around 65 liters per second on average.

This is because the grooves in the tread and the tire channels can allow water to flow quickly, avoiding the phenomenon known as aquaplaning, which occurs when a layer of water accumulates between the track surface and the tire tread, causing a loss of contact between them and reducing vehicle traction and control.

In races with heavy rain, drivers may be forced to switch to extreme wet weather tires, which are even deeper and have even more channels to allow water to flow.

These tires are used only in very specific situations of heavy rain and are not suitable for mixed or dry conditions.

44

The telemetry system is used in Formula 1 to collect real-time information on the performance of the car and the behavior of the driver during the race.

Telemetry is gathered through a variety of sensors placed in different parts of the car, such as the tires, brakes, engine, and suspension.

The data is transmitted from the car to the team's garage through a high-speed wireless network, and is recorded and analyzed in real-time to help engineers make strategic decisions about the car's performance.

Telemetry data is also used to conduct simulations and tests in the lab to improve the design of the car.

The amount of data collected during a race is truly impressive.

According to some reports, up to 1,000 channels of data can be recorded per second, which equates to over 4 million data points per lap.

The team's engineers use this data to adjust the car's settings in real-time and optimize the performance of the car in the race.

45

The exhaust pipes of Formula 1 cars often reach very high temperatures due to the high speeds at which they travel and the heat generated by the engine.

In fact, it is estimated that the temperature of the gases that come out of the engine can exceed 1,000 degrees Celsius.

This high temperature is capable of melting metals and materials that are not designed to withstand it, so exhaust pipes are made of special materials that can withstand high temperatures.

In addition, cooling and insulation systems are also used to prevent the temperature of the exhaust pipes from affecting other parts of the car.

46

During the Formula 1 race on the urban circuit of Monaco, sewer covers can come loose due to the high aerodynamic suction generated by the single-seaters.

To prevent this, the maintenance teams of the city of Monaco weld the covers to ensure they don't come off during the race.

This is one of the special challenges of racing on an urban circuit, where cars compete on narrow and winding streets that are normally open to public traffic.

The Monaco Grand Prix is considered one of the most prestigious and exciting of the season due to its history, location, and unique challenges on the track.

47

In the history of Formula 1, there was an experiment with six-wheeled cars.

The idea behind this was that by having more wheels on the ground, the contact surface could be increased and therefore improve traction and grip in corners.

The first six-wheeled car to compete in Formula 1 was the March 2-4-0 in 1976, followed by the Tyrrell P34 in 1977.

The Tyrrell P34 became the most famous of them all due to its success in the 1976 season.

The car was equipped with four small front wheels, two on each side, which reduced air resistance and increased the contact surface with the ground.

Additionally, the car had a very innovative chassis that helped maintain stability in corners.

Despite its success, six-wheeled cars did not last long in Formula 1.

The FIA, the governing body of the competition, decided to ban them starting from the 1983 season, arguing that the use of four front wheels gave an unfair aerodynamic advantage to the teams that used them.

48

Nowadays, Formula 1 drivers tend to debut at younger ages than in the past, but there are still some cases of veteran drivers who continue to compete.

For example, in the 2021 season, Kimi Raikkonen was 41 years old and Fernando Alonso was 39 years old at the time of his return to the category.

Regarding Luigi Fagioli's record, it is true that he was the oldest driver to win a Formula 1 Grand Prix.

He did it at the 1951 French Grand Prix, at the age of 53 years and 22 days.

However, it is important to note that at that time Formula 1 was not like we know it today, as it was contested under the rules of the Grand Prix Formula, which allowed the participation of cars from different categories and there was no world championship as such.

49

Formula 1 is one of the most popular and media-covered sports in the world, with a large number of followers globally.

The audience for Formula 1 has remained stable in some places, but has decreased in others in recent years due to a variety of factors, such as the lack of excitement in the races and the proliferation of pay channels that make it difficult to access the broadcast of the events.

Despite this, it is estimated that Formula 1 has around 400 million followers worldwide, which is still an impressive figure.

However, compared to a decade ago, the audience has decreased significantly, as at that time Formula 1 was estimated to be followed by over 500 million viewers.

Formula 1 is broadcast in more than 200 countries and regions worldwide, making it one of the most globalized sports in the world.

As the sport continues to evolve, Formula 1 seeks new ways to attract viewers, from the inclusion of new races on the calendar to the use of new technologies to enhance the spectator experience.

50

Formula 1 cars generate a significant amount of aerodynamic downforce at high speeds, allowing them to stick to the ground and take corners at high speeds.

In fact, at speeds above 160 km/h, the aerodynamic downforce generated can be equal to or even greater than the weight of the car.

However, this does not mean that the car can stay on the roof of a tunnel and be driven upside down, as the aerodynamic downforce only works in a specific direction and the car is designed to stay on its four wheels in contact with the track.

Additionally, the weight of the engine and other parts of the car also contribute to the total weight, so the aerodynamic downforce is not enough to counteract all of the weight of the car in all situations.

In summary, while Formula 1 cars are capable of generating large amounts of aerodynamic downforce, they cannot be driven upside down on the roof of a tunnel.

51

Where did the history of F1 begin?

In 1946, just a year after the end of World War II, the Fédération Internationale de l'Automobile (FIA) began to consider the idea of a single-seater category to unify all the existing national Grand Prix series into a single Drivers' Championship.

When the Motorcycle World Championship appeared in 1949, the FIA responded by creating the Formula One World Championship, which began in 1950.

Initially, the Indianapolis 500 was part of the championship but it was removed in 1960 because its rules didn't fit with those of F1.

Excluding Indianapolis, there were no F1 Grand Prix outside Europe until 1953, when Argentina joined.

Since then, there has always been at least one race outside the old continent and since 1958 there has also been a Constructors' World Championship.

52

The first race of the F1 World Championship was held on 13 May 1950 at Silverstone UK.

The British Grand Prix had started again in 1948, after two races in the 1920s and the construction of the new Silverstone circuit on a disused airfield.

The fifth year of Silverstone was the first qualifying round of the F1 Drivers' World Championship.

This and the Italian Grand Prix are the only two that have never been missing from the calendar, albeit sometimes under the name of the European Grand Prix.

The winner of the first F1 race was Italian driver Giuseppe Farina (Nino Farina).

53

As well as winning the first race, Farina was the first F1 World Champion, at the wheel of an Alfa Romeo after taking three of the seven victories of the season.

Despite his success, in 1951, Juan Manuel Fangio was the team's best driver and Farina had to take a back seat.

Things did not improve after his departure to Ferrari, where Alberto Ascari outperformed him by far.

He won his fifth and last race at the 1953 German Grand Prix.

1950 was the only World Championship he won.

54

Michael Schumacher.

To date, Schumacher's seven titles have never been beaten.

His titles in 1994, 1995, 2000, 2001, 2002, 2003 and 2004 is not the only record the German holds: he also has the most victories in F1 history, with ninety-one.

He has also stood on the podium more than any other driver having done so 155 times and in 2002 he finished in the top three in all seventeen races.

He is the only driver to have finished every the podium in a single season.

55

Juan Manuel Fangio.

The only Argentinean F1 champion, with five titles, all won in the 1950s.

He has the highest winning percentage in history, with 46.15% (24 victories in 52 races), well above Alberto Ascari's 39.39% and Jim Clark's 34.25%.

He also has the Best Pole Position Percentage at 55.77%, in twenty-nine races out of fifty-two.

Not bad for someone who was on the verge of abandoning his career behind the wheel!

56

Which year was the most closely fought F1 World Championship?

When it comes to points difference, the tightest of all was 1984.

Niki Lauda won the title by only a half point over his teammate Alain Prost.

This half point was from the Monaco Grand Prix, which was cancelled due to rain and where only half points were awarded.

What about the Championship that was decided in the shortest time?

That was undoubtedly in 2008, when Felipe Massa crossed the finish line of the Brazilian Grand Prix.

His rival was sixth, one place behind the position needed to take the championship.

While the entire circuit was celebrating his compatriot's title by thirty-nine seconds Lewis Hamilton crossed the finish line in fifth place after overtaking Timo Glock on the last corner and could have become F1 World Champion for the first time.

57

Up to 2018, more than a hundred teams have competed in the F1 World Championship, often under different names over various periods.

The oldest, and the only one that has been present in every season of the premier class, is Ferrari.

Ferrari's first Grand Prix was at Monaco 1950, the second qualifying round of F1.

Since then, Ferrari has only missed a few races and has won the most constructors' titles, the most races, and the most victories, podiums and pole positions: and it keeps on adding up.

Many teams have come and gone because of the cost: Bugatti was only on the grid once, and Porsche, only won a single race, back in 1962.

Others came back after leaving, like Mercedes, which after the Le Mans Tragedy and the FIA's decision not to stop the race, left F1 for fifty-five years.

58

Some technological advances that marked an epoch and revolutionised the sport at the time:

-The rear-mounted engine: Its point of no return began with the 1958 Cooper, despite the reluctance of leading lights such as Enzo Ferrari.

-The monocoque chassis: First used by Lotus in 1962 and made from a single sheet of aluminium.

-Wings: inspired by those used in Gran Turismo and by Lotus and first used at the 1968 Monaco Grand Prix.

-Ground Effect: once again it was Lotus who revolutionised the sport. In 1977, ground effect got drivers onto the top of the podium five times.

-Carbon Fibre Chassis: McLaren introduced it in 1981, despite doubts about its crash safety. That same year, John Watson walked away from a crash that could have resulted in serious injury or death, had it not been for this innovation. Gradually, carbon began to make inroads, not only because it was safer, lighter and stiffer, but it improved grip and cornering speed.

59

An engine has about five thousand parts, of which around one thousand five hundred are moving.

Before they were limited to eight hundred horsepower, an engine could top 1000 and reach 20,000 rpm.

Today's F1 engines produce around 720 hp, from a V8, limited to 19,000 rpm.

Their aluminium alloy construction provides lightness and strength and while other more advanced materials like composites and super alloys would certainly reduce weight, to keep costs down as much as possible, the FIA has banned non-ferrous materials.

60

**F1 engines produce around
1,750 kW a minute.**

This amount of heat must be expelled somehow, through the radiators and the exhaust, which can reach temperatures of up to 550°C and consume about seventy-five litres per 100 km, a F1 engine is twenty per cent more efficient than a car engine.

As for reliability and durability, they only have to last for a certain number of Grand Prix races according to the regulations of that season, otherwise the driver is penalised according to the FIA rules.

At maximum engine speed (around 18,000 rpm), a F1 engine consumes 0.4 kilograms of air a second, that's 24 kilograms a minute, enough to inflate 600 balloons.

61

Formula 1 engines are marvels of engineering and represent the pinnacle of automotive technology.

Exhaust Sound: Formula 1 engines are known for their distinctive and powerful roar. Unlike regular vehicles, which have muffler systems to reduce noise, F1 cars have no such constraints. This lack of a muffler, combined with the high revolutions at which these engines operate, results in an unmistakable sound that can be heard from great distances on a track.

Gearboxes: The performance and durability of the gearbox are vital in Formula 1. During a race, an F1 driver can make thousands of gear changes. These gearboxes are designed to be highly resistant and efficient. Unlike standard cars that might have a brief delay between shifts, the sequential gearboxes of F1 cars allow for nearly instantaneous changes, crucial for maintaining optimal speeds and consistent performance.

Shift Frequency: On some circuits, the nature of the layout demands frequent gear shifts. For instance, in the Canadian Grand Prix, drivers shift gears at an astonishing rate, approximately once every 1.3 seconds. This would be inconceivable in a traditional manual vehicle and highlights the impressive skill and endurance of the drivers, as well as the efficiency of the F1 gearboxes.

62

Lubrication is a crucial aspect of the operation of any engine, but in Formula 1 engines, given their extremely demanding conditions, it is of utmost importance.

Importance of Lubrication: In an F1 engine, parts move at incredibly high speeds and pressures. These moving parts generate friction, and without proper lubrication, this friction can cause excessive wear and even catastrophic damage to the engine. Moreover, due to the high speeds and G-forces involved, oil can be pushed to one side of the engine, potentially leaving other parts of the engine without adequate lubrication.

Pump System: The seven oil pumps work together to ensure that oil reaches all vital parts of the engine. Their design and efficient operation showcase the precision and advanced engineering behind F1. Despite their critical role, these pumps are surprisingly energy-efficient.

Oil Layer: The 20 μm (micrometers) oil layer highlights the precision with which lubrication is handled in these engines. Such a thin layer of oil means that lubrication is extremely efficient, allowing the parts to move freely without unnecessary resistance. When compared to the thickness of a human hair, which typically measures between 40 and 50 μm, one can appreciate how fine this oil coating is.

63

Michael Schumacher is considered one of the most successful drivers in the history of Formula 1, having won seven world titles and 91 races throughout his career.

He is the Formula 1 driver who has earned the most money in his career.

According to Forbes, Schumacher amassed earnings worth $1 billion in his Formula 1 career, thanks to his salaries, bonuses, and sponsorships.

Other drivers like Lewis Hamilton and Fernando Alonso have also earned large sums of money in their careers, but they have not yet reached the total amount accumulated by Schumacher.

Schumacher was sponsored by brands such as Ferrari, Mercedes-Benz, Omega, and Nescafé, and he also had investments in properties and other businesses.

64

The brake discs of F1 cars are made of indestructible carbon fibre and can reach 1,000 degrees Celsius, the same temperature as molten lava.

Extreme braking produces sufficient force that the driver's tear ducts leak tears! Brake discs have improved enormously over the years, and engineers are pushing the limits of what was considered impossible just a decade ago.

In 2016, attempts were made to drill 1,200 holes in a single brake disc to cool the air, which can get extremely hot.

F1 brake discs had around a hundred holes a couple of years ago.

65

Formula 1 engines are extremely advanced and are specifically designed for the unique conditions of high-performance racing.

Preheating: F1 engines operate within very specific temperature ranges. When cold, the oil and other fluids within the engine become more viscous, which can restrict the movement of internal parts and increase the risk of damage. Preheating the engine helps these fluids reach a proper consistency and ensures all parts move with the least resistance possible.

Tight Tolerances: F1 engines are built with extremely tight tolerances to maximize efficiency and performance. However, these tight tolerances can pose problems if parts aren't in ideal conditions. For instance, when metal is cold, it contracts, and in an engine with such precise tolerances, this could lead to a misfit of components.

Gearbox: Just like the engine, an F1 car's gearbox also has very tight tolerances and performs best at specific temperatures. If the gearbox isn't warm enough, shifting gears effectively and without damaging the equipment can be challenging.

Adaptation Challenges: The need for preheating and the specific demands of F1 engines and gearboxes mean they can't just be installed into a regular car and expected to operate. These units are designed for a very particular purpose and have unique requirements not found in most road vehicles.

66

A typical family car engine runs at about 6,000 RPM, but a F1 car runs at well over three times that because of its enormous power output.

Naturally aspirated engines for F1 cars didn't change much over the years.

Prior to the '80s, most F1 engines were limited to 12,000 RPM because the valves were operated with metal springs, but once Renault developed pneumatic valves, development was rapid.

All F1 engines now use pneumatic valves and are enormously high revving, redlining at 20,000 RPM.

67

A F1 car combines more than 80,000 components.

All of these components must be precisely assembled if the car is to perform as expected.

Every highly engineered piece has a function and has been thought out down to the last detail and while an F1 car may look simple to an outsider, it takes thousands of hours and huge resources to create one.

There is a 99.9 per cent requirement that components are repairable accurately for the car to perform optimally: there is no margin for error when it comes to a F1 car.

68

A F1 engine can only be used for five races and so teams apportion a considerable budget just for engine development.

The engine of a F1 car is not like the typical one found in a Toyota that will give you 200,000 miles of faithful motoring without missing a beat.

The tolerance and performance of F1 engines are on another level and they have been painstakingly designed to give maximum performance, even at the cost of only giving it for a few hours.

The extreme precision involved in their construction subjects them to enormous wear and tear in their short lifetime.

69

Formula 1 cars are masterful examples of engineering and design.

While lightness is a sought-after trait in these vehicles to enhance their speed and maneuverability, it's also essential that they have the right weight and balance to ensure stability and safety on the track.

Construction Materials: Composite carbon fiber is a primary choice in the construction of F1 cars due to its remarkable strength-to-weight ratio. It is incredibly durable and lightweight, meaning it can provide the necessary structural integrity for a race car while minimizing the overall weight.

Minimum Weight Requirement: The 728 KG threshold for F1 cars, including their dry weather tires, isn't an arbitrary figure. It's a standard set by the FIA (International Automobile Federation) to ensure a level playing field among teams and enhance safety. If all cars have similar weights, it eliminates any potential advantage that a significantly lighter car might have in terms of acceleration and handling.

Use of Ballast: Prior to 2014, due to regulations and the design of the vehicles, many cars couldn't meet the minimum weight requirement on their own. Instead of altering the car's fundamental design or using heavier materials, teams added ballast to the vehicle. The advantage of ballast is its flexibility: it can be placed in strategic locations to optimize weight distribution. For instance, if a car tends to be heavier at the back, ballast could be added to the front to balance the weight distribution.

Center of Gravity and Stability: The center of gravity is a crucial concept in vehicle dynamics. A lower center of gravity makes the car more stable, reducing the risk of tipping and enhancing traction and cornering ability. By being able to adjust the ballast's location, teams can manipulate the car's center of gravity, ensuring it's in an optimal position for a track's specific characteristics or race conditions.

70

**These cars are not just about
speed and performance.**

They are one of the safest cars to drive in
the world, although they are notoriously
uncomfortable and it takes enormous
stamina to race one for hours.

There have been many accidents over the
years, although rarely nowadays
are they fatal.

An F1 driver can survive the impact of going
from a hundred miles an hour to a dead stop
in two seconds and the cars must pass an
exhaustive list of safety checks before
being allowed to race.

The driver's cockpit must be as safe
as possible.

71

**The greatest risk of injury is head
and neck trauma.**

F1 strives to mitigate these types of injury by
setting exacting standards for the helmets
that drivers wear, the first of which is that
they must be ultra-lightweight.

This presents the challenge of building them
as strong as possible, while meeting weight
restrictions.

To ensure that the helmets meet the strict
requirements, they must undergo a battery
of fragmentation and deformation tests.

Carbon fibre is the principal material used
because of its strength and the outer shell
is in two layers, with carbon fibre making
up the majority of the material.

72

The Albert Park circuit is located in Melbourne, Australia and was specifically designed to host Formula 1 races.

It was opened in 1996 and has since been the circuit that hosts the Australian Grand Prix, the first event of the Formula 1 season.

The circuit is located within the park of the same name and has a length of 5.303 kilometers and 16 corners.

It is an urban circuit that uses the streets of the city of Melbourne to create a fast and technical layout that tests the skills of the drivers.

Over the years, the Albert Park circuit has been the scene of some memorable races, such as Damon Hill's victory in 1996 in the first Grand Prix held at the circuit, the exciting 2002 race in which Mark Webber achieved a historic fifth place for the Minardi team, or Kimi Raikkonen's victory in 2013 after starting from seventh on the grid.

Due to the COVID-19 pandemic, the Formula 1 Australian Grand Prix was canceled in 2020 and 2021.

73

The local factor can have an impact on the performance and motivation of Formula 1 drivers.

Drivers may feel greater pressure when competing in their home country or on a circuit that is familiar and particularly enjoyable to them.

In addition, the local fans can cheer and support the drivers of their country, which can increase their confidence and motivation.

On the other hand, there are also cases where the pressure and expectations of the local fans can negatively affect the drivers, making them feel overwhelmed and unable to perform at their best.

Each circuit has its own particularities and unique characteristics, which can benefit some teams and drivers over others.

For example, a driver who is familiar with a circuit that has many slow corners may have an advantage over a driver who prefers faster and more straight circuits.

Overall, the local factor can have an impact on the performance of drivers, but it also depends on many other factors such as the physical and mental condition of the driver, the performance of the car, and the strategy of the team.

For example, Jenson Button acknowledged that for him and any British driver, racing at Silverstone is the most anticipated moment of the year.

The same can be said for Italian drivers when they race at Monza.

74

Nutrition is a fundamental part of a driver's preparation for race day, not only to ensure they have enough energy to compete but also to maintain focus and avoid fatigue.

Breakfast: It's essential to start the day with energy. Drivers often consume protein-rich foods, such as eggs or yogurt, and combine them with antioxidant and vitamin-rich fruits, like berries or kiwi. It's also common to add whole grains to provide a sustained energy source.

Pre-race Meal: The meal before the race shouldn't be too heavy, to avoid feeling full or sluggish. Foods rich in lean proteins like chicken, fish, or legumes, accompanied by steamed vegetables or salads, are ideal choices. While some drivers may avoid carbohydrates, others opt for complex carbs, such as quinoa or brown rice, to provide a gradual release of energy.

Hydration: As mentioned, drivers consume large amounts of water before and during the race. It's also common for them to drink isotonic beverages that replenish lost electrolytes from sweating. Dehydration can severely affect concentration and muscle function, so staying hydrated is essential.

Post-race: After the race, it's vital to replenish lost nutrients and fluids. A balanced meal that combines proteins, carbohydrates, and healthy fats is ideal.
Protein shakes are also popular to aid in muscle recovery.

75

F1 drivers are among the most conditioned athletes in the world, not only for their ability to drive at extreme speeds but also for the incredible physical and mental endurance the sport demands.

G-forces and Muscle Endurance: Drivers experience G-forces multiple times during a race, especially during hard braking and fast turns. This means their body can feel as if it weighs up to five times its normal weight. To cope with these forces, drivers need to have extremely strong neck, shoulder, and torso muscles.

Cardiovascular Endurance: Cardiovascular training is crucial. Races are grueling, and the combination of high temperatures inside the single-seater and the intensity of the competition can cause a driver's heart rate to reach very high levels. Keeping a strong and healthy heart is essential to ensure they can keep pace throughout the race without tiring.

Reflexes and Mental Agility: At the high speeds that single-seaters reach, drivers need to make decisions in split seconds. This requires great mental agility, complemented by specific exercises and driving simulators to enhance hand-eye coordination and reaction times.

Flexibility: Flexibility is also essential, especially to maneuver within the tight cockpit of the single-seater and to prevent injuries.

Altitude Training: Some drivers choose to train at high altitudes to enhance their lung and cardiovascular capacity, which can be especially beneficial on circuits located at high elevations, like the Autódromo Hermanos Rodríguez in Mexico City.

76

Schumacher vs. Hill

In the mid-1990s, the Kaiser met his first great rival in F1, Damon Hill.

Their rivalry came about in dramatic fashion, as the Briton took lead drive in the Williams team after the death of Ayrton Senna at Imola (1994) and fought for the title against the German right down to the last race in Australia.

As with Senna and Prost, the outcome was unforgettable.

The Antipodean race was the scene of a collision which sent Schumacher careering into the tyre wall, while Hill suffered suspension damage that forced him to retire.

The FIA found no fault with Schumacher, who nudged ahead by a single point, taking the championship.

Hill had his revenge in '96 though, taking the title from Schumacher, who had just finished his first year at Ferrari and was yet to find the form that made him a legend later on.

77

Mansell vs. Piquet.

The Williams team was the victim of the power struggle between Nigel Mansell and Nelson Piquet throughout the 80s.

They never got on well together and the Brazilian had a number of slanging matches with his team-mate and rival.

Despite the tension, there were never any serious incidents between the two on the track so at least sportsmanship reigned where it was most needed, and there were many beautiful duels such as the one at Silverstone in '87.

However, the Briton suffered accidents at Spa and Suzuka as a result of the tension between the two, which cost him a broken vertebra, enabling Piquet to become champion.

78

Schumacher vs. Hakkinen.

Another healthy on-track rivalry was that between Michael Schumacher and Mika Hakkinen, at the turn of the century.

Ferrari and McLaren had been battling it out for the title, but things came to a head at Silverstone in '99 when Schumi broke his right leg after a head-on shunt with the crash barriers and was out for the rest of the year.

One particularly memorable overtake was by the Finn at Spa in 2000, when he slipstreamed the lapped Ricardo Zonta to pass both of them.

Of course, it was Schumacher who had the last laugh. In his own words, Hakkinen was the only rival he feared.

79

Verstappen vs. Hamilton.

2021 saw the start of the real rivalry between the Dutchman and the British seven-time champion.

Before that, they had been swapping victories, but Red Bull closed up on Mercedes and that led to real head-to-head duels between the two, which peaked at Silverstone, Monza and Saudi Arabia, with Verstappen crashing into the barriers and into the air, as well as having to drop a place and take a hit from the Englishman.

In fact, in the second of these, if it wasn't for the Halo, Hamilton would probably not be here today, as his car flipped.

Finally, in Abu Dhabi, in another heart-stopping outcome, Verstappen stole victory and what was to be Hamilton's eighth championship.

80

Maggotts-Becketts-Chapel-Silverstone.

All these corners are in the cradle of the championship, Silverstone.

Their enormous popularity is because of the physical demands that 3Gs place on the drivers as they hurtle through them.

The fast left-right-left-left-right-left turns require the precision of a watchmaker at around three hundred kilometres an hour, and in between they have to drop a gear and then charge down the Hangar Straight all the way to Stowe.

The difficulty of making it through them unscathed at the start of a Grand Prix is enormous, so it's hardly surprising that it is the most emblematic section of the English circuit.

81

Eau Rouge – Spa Francorchamps.

The Spa-Francorchamps circuit is one of the favourites of many drivers on the grid for its speed and overtaking opportunities.

The high point is the Eau Rouge corner, at the back of the first very tight corner where the main straight ends.

It climbs steeply through the Ardennes forest and subjects the drivers to 4Gs before accelerating hard down the straight.

The great Ayrton Senna used to say that he prayed to god every time he went through it.

Mikka Hakkinen's most memorable overtake here was when he slipstreamed past Ricardo Zonta and Michael Schumacher in 2000.

82

The Parabolica/Alboreto – Monza.

Monza is called the temple of speed thanks to the straights that form the backbone of the circuit.

It is spiced up by its bends that the drivers charge down flat out; one of these is the Parabolica, the last corner before hitting the finish straight.

It's a wide radius turn of about 180 degrees, preceded by the straight that begins at Ascari and the key is to find the line to exit flat out towards the straight.

Charles Leclerc in 2020 and Austrian Jochen Rindt in free practice in 1970 both went into the wall at enormous speed after losing control, so it's not without its difficulties.

83

Loews – Monaco.

This list would not be complete without Monaco, and we've included the slowest corner along its 3.337 metres: Loews.

The hairpin sits right by the luxurious Fairmont Hotel, entered at around just sixty kilometres an hour, with a vicious 180-degree angle, forcing the teams to widen the turning circle of the car.

There have been countless contacts during overtakes here like 2008 when Fernando Alonso tried to overtake Nick Heidfeld and touched his left rear wheel, resulting in a major pile-up and damaging the front wing of his Renault.

84

130R – Suzuka.

Suzuka has been the scene of many key moments in F1 history.

The 130R is the straight that comes into the last chicane before the main straight of the Japanese track and is where the drivers reach the highest top speed.

Its name comes from its radius, with a left-hand turn taken flat out.

It was here that Alonso made his great overtake on Michael Schumacher in 2005 when he already had the title in his pocket, forcing his way around the outside to take the inside line on the chicane.

85

The Wall of Champions - Gilles Villeneuve.

Although the Gilles Villeneuve circuit is not exactly brimming with famous corners, the last one is famous enough.

The Wall of Champions is at the start of the Canadian track's finish straight and comes just after the final chicane, a right-left that spits the drivers into it.

Its reputation was born at the '99 Canadian Grand Prix, when it was touched on the same weekend by three world champions: Damon Hill (1996), Michael Schumacher (1994 and 1995) and the track's namesake's son, Jaques Villeneuve (1997).

It later claimed Sebastian Vettel in 2011 in his Red Bull, which speaks volumes about how demanding it is.

86

The Senna S - Interlagos.

The home of one of the greatest drivers of all time, Ayrton Senna, boasts a corner worthy of mention, more for its peculiarity and to whom it pays tribute than anything else, but the sweep of the Senna S with its downhill slope deserves a mention here.

These are the first corners the drivers encounter after starting, first left and then right, before heading onto the Oposta straight.

Among the most memorable overtakes is Juan Pablo Montoya's move on Michael Schumacher in 2001, when he got inside the Kaiser and closed the gap on him at the second turn to overtake.

Carlos Sainz also had to take a huge risk just here to get his first podium in 2019 coming from behind.

87

Tamburello at Imola.

The Imola Circuit, officially known as the Autodromo Enzo e Dino Ferrari, is located in Italy and has been the venue for numerous Formula 1 Grand Prix over the years.

One of the most iconic and, at the same time, most infamous sections of this circuit is the Tamburello curve.

History and tragedies: Until 1994, Tamburello was a fast left-hand curve that drivers took at full speed.

However, this curve became tragically famous during the 1994 San Marino Grand Prix due to two fatal accidents.

The first occurred during Saturday practice when Austrian driver Roland Ratzenberger lost control of his car, crashing into the barriers.

Despite medical efforts, Ratzenberger died from the injuries sustained in the accident.

The following day, during the race, Ayrton Senna, one of the most iconic and beloved drivers in Formula 1, had an accident at the same Tamburello curve.

His Williams violently collided with the retaining wall.

Despite the swift intervention of medical teams, Senna passed away shortly after due to his injuries.

Modifications to the circuit: Following the tragic events of 1994, significant modifications were made to the Imola circuit to enhance safety.

One of the most crucial changes was the introduction of a chicane at the Tamburello curve to reduce speeds and increase safety in that area.

This chicane consists of a series of turns: first to the left, then to the right, and finally back to the left, similar to the Ascari variant in Monza.

88

Nouvelle Chicane – Monaco.

The end of the Monaco tunnel straight is called the Nouvelle Chicane and is practically the only possible overtaking point along the entire track.

Drivers hurtle into it at around two hundred and fifty kilometres an hour, and along the way, there is a wall that is often brushed as the cars fly down towards it.

The view is breath-taking, with the Mediterranean and the port of the Monegasque Principality in the background, and has been the scene of many overtakes, although none more memorable than in 2010, when Fernando Alonso put on a great show, coming back from the pits to finish sixth after a huge impact that damaged the chassis of his Ferrari.

89

Pouhon - Spa Francorchamps.

Pouhon is a corner of the Spa-Francorchamps circuit located in Belgium, which is located in the forest section.

It is a fast corner taken downhill and drivers must take it at full throttle at speeds over 300 km/h.

It is a very demanding and technical corner due to its complexity and the high amount of G-forces experienced by the drivers at this point of the circuit.

It is called Pouhon after a spring located nearby that has medicinal properties.

In addition to Pouhon, Spa-Francorchamps is known for being one of the most challenging circuits in Formula 1 due to its high-speed corners and mountainous terrain.

It is also famous for the long Kemmel straight, where cars reach speeds of over 300 km/h.

90

Senna vs. Prost.

The duels between the Brazilian and the Frenchman throughout the 1980s and early 1990s were legendary.

Both were legendary drivers in their own ways: Senna was more aggressive and unbeatable in the rain, while Prost shied away from conflict on the track with elegant driving.

They shared a garage during their time at McLaren, so the beginning of their enmity can possibly be traced back to 1988, when Senna signed for the British team, where Prost was already king.

Unlike nowadays, Prost actually lobbied for Senna to be signed so few could have imagined what happened afterwards.

They were both extremely competitive, and that finally exploded within the team.

Before the end of their partnership there was a championship ending that any fan who saw it will never forget.

91

Alonso vs. Hamilton.

Although there were no ugly scenes between them, the McLaren partnership of Fernando Alonso and Lewis Hamilton again made history, even though they only spent a year together.

The Spaniard arrived as the new dominator of the championship on the back of his two titles in the previous years with Renault.

The Briton, on the other hand, came to F1 after having won the GP2 World Championship, the prelude to the Great Circus.

At first glance, one would have thought that one would have been the other's teacher but nothing could have been further from the truth.

Everything seemed to be going smoothly until the 2007 Monaco Grand Prix, where Alonso dominated from start to finish, but Hamilton got on his tail on the final straight with the intention of overtaking, but it was blocked by the team manager.

After all, they were on for an assured one-two and risking anything in the Principality can be costly.

92

Lauda vs. Hunt.

A rivalry fit for Hollywood! The film Rush tells the story.

Between them they set the pace of the championship in the '70s, and it was in the middle of the decade, in 1976, that it reached its peak, the season depicted in the film, which saw the Austrian win four of the first six races and take two second places, while the Briton had four retirements.

It all looked set to be another title for the Ferrari driver, but for that dreadful fiery crash at the Nürburgring, which almost ended his life changed everything.

93

Lance Stroll won €8,500,000.

He is a Canadian racing driver who currently competes in Formula 1 for the Aston Martin team.

Stroll was born on October 29, 1998, in Montreal, Canada, and is the son of billionaire Lawrence Stroll, who owns the Formula 1 team Racing Point (now Aston Martin).

Lance Stroll began his career in karting in 2008 and won several championships in Canada and the United States before moving to the Italian Formula 4 in 2014.

In 2015, he competed in the European Formula 3 and in 2016, won the European Formula 3 championship with Prema Powerteam.

In 2017, Stroll made his Formula 1 debut with Williams, where he competed for two seasons before joining Racing Point (now Aston Martin) in 2019.

Stroll has achieved a couple of podiums in his Formula 1 career and a pole position in the Turkish Grand Prix in 2020.

According to the French magazine Auto Hebdo, Stroll earned around €8.5 million in salary and bonuses in the 2020 Formula 1 season, however, it should be mentioned that Formula 1 driver salaries are private information and not officially confirmed.

94

Valtteri Bottas won €8,500,000.

He is a Finnish Formula 1 driver who currently races for the Alfa Romeo Racing team.

Prior to his arrival at Alfa Romeo in the 2022 season, Bottas had spent the last five years at the Mercedes team, where he had been the teammate of Lewis Hamilton and had helped Mercedes win several constructor championships.

During his time at Mercedes, Bottas won a total of nine races, including three in the 2020 season.

He also achieved 17 pole positions and 17 fastest laps during his career with Mercedes.

His best result in the championship standings was second place in 2019 and 2020, behind his teammate Lewis Hamilton.

Prior to his arrival in Formula 1, Bottas had won the Formula 3 Euroseries championship in 2011 and had been a test driver for the Williams team in 2012.

He made his Formula 1 debut with Williams in 2013 and spent four years with the team before his move to Mercedes.

According to the 2021 Formula 1 salary list published by Business Book GP, Bottas earned an annual salary of €8.5 million in his last season with Mercedes.

95

Carlos Sainz earned €8,500,000.

He is a Spanish Formula 1 driver who has competed for various teams throughout his career, including Toro Rosso, Renault, McLaren, and Ferrari.

In 2021, Sainz joined the Ferrari team to replace German driver Sebastian Vettel.

In his first year with Ferrari, Sainz performed well, achieving four podium finishes during the season, including a second-place finish at the Monaco Grand Prix and a third-place finish at the Italian Grand Prix.

He also managed to outscore his teammate, Charles Leclerc, in the final championship standings.

Regarding his salary, it is estimated that Carlos Sainz earned €8.5 million during the 2021 Formula 1 season.

96

Charles Leclerc earned €8,500,000.

He is a Monegasque driver who currently competes for the Ferrari Formula 1 team.

He was born on October 16, 1997, in Monte Carlo and began his career in karting at the age of 8.

In 2014, he made his debut in single-seaters in the Formula Renault 2.0, where he finished runner-up in his first season.

After competing in the European Formula 3 and Formula 2, Leclerc made his Formula 1 debut in 2018 with the Sauber team (now Alfa Romeo Racing).

In his first year, he put in a notable performance, scoring points in 10 races and achieving a best result of sixth place in Azerbaijan.

In 2019, he was hired by Ferrari, replacing Kimi Raikkonen, and achieved two victories (Belgium and Italy) and seven podium finishes in his first season with the team.

In 2020, Ferrari had a poor performance and Leclerc had less success, but he still managed to score two podium finishes and a pole position.

Regarding his salary, during the 2021 season, Leclerc earned €8.5 million, the same as his teammates Carlos Sainz and Valtteri Bottas.

97

Daniel Ricciardo earned €13,000,000.

He is a Formula 1 driver born in Australia on July 1, 1989.

He began his career in Formula Renault and then progressed to Formula 3 before making his Formula 1 debut with the HRT team in 2011.

In 2012, he joined Toro Rosso, Red Bull Racing's sister team, before being promoted to Red Bull in 2014.

With Red Bull, Ricciardo achieved seven wins and 29 podiums in five seasons, becoming one of the sport's most prominent drivers.

In 2019, he switched to Renault, where he had a difficult season and did not achieve any wins or podiums.

In 2021, he joined McLaren, where he won his first race in three years at the Italian Grand Prix in Monza.

As for his salary, it is estimated that Ricciardo earned €13 million in 2021 with McLaren.

His contract with the team is for several years, and he is expected to remain a competitive driver in the future.

Outside of the track, Ricciardo is known for his outgoing personality and his love of extreme sports such as skydiving and snowboarding.

98

Sebastian Vettel earned €13,000,000.

He is a German Formula 1 driver who made his debut in the category in 2007 with BMW Sauber, although his true breakthrough came in 2008 when he joined Red Bull Racing.

With this team, Vettel achieved his four consecutive world championships between 2010 and 2013, becoming one of the most successful and highly paid drivers in F1 history.

In 2015, Vettel joined the Scuderia Ferrari, where he spent six seasons, achieving a total of 14 wins and 54 podiums.

In 2021, Vettel changed teams and joined Aston Martin (formerly Racing Point), where he currently competes.

In addition to his four world championships, Vettel is also known for his skill on the track, his aggressiveness, and his ability to lead a team.

He is one of the most successful drivers of his generation and has left an indelible mark on F1.

99

Fernando Alonso won €17.5 million.

He is a Spanish driver who has had a successful career in Formula 1.

He won two world championships in 2005 and 2006 with the Renault team, and has competed for other major teams such as McLaren, Ferrari, and now Alpine F1 Team.

He is known for his skill on the track, his ability to take risks, and his ability to overcome difficulties in race situations.

In 2018, Alonso announced that he would retire from Formula 1 after the season, but returned in 2021 with Alpine, the former Renault team.

As you mentioned, in his comeback he achieved a podium in Qatar and showed his skill in Hungary, where he defended his position against Lewis Hamilton for several laps.

In addition to his success in Formula 1, Alonso has also competed in other major motorsport events, including the FIA World Endurance Championship and the 24 Hours of Le Mans, in which he has won both.

He has also competed in the Indy 500 and won the 24 Hours of Daytona.

As for his salary, as you mentioned, it is estimated that he earned €17.5 million in 2021, making him one of the highest paid drivers on the grid.

100

Max Verstappen won €22 million.

He is a Dutch Formula 1 driver who currently races for Red Bull Racing.

He was born on September 30, 1997 in Hasselt, Belgium, but holds Dutch nationality.

He is the son of former Formula 1 driver Jos Verstappen.

Max Verstappen made his Formula 1 debut in 2015 with the Toro Rosso team, becoming the youngest driver in the history of the category at just 17 years old.

The following year, in 2016, he was promoted to Red Bull Racing, where he quickly became one of the most promising drivers on the grid.

Verstappen has achieved a total of 20 wins, 46 podiums, and 10 pole positions in his Formula 1 career.

In 2021, he became world champion for the first time, surpassing seven-time champion Lewis Hamilton in an exciting and controversial season.

In addition to his skill on the track, Verstappen has stood out for his personality off it.

He is considered a very aggressive and daring driver, and has generated controversy on several occasions for his driving style.

He has also demonstrated to be a very shrewd driver in race strategy, and has been praised for his ability to maintain concentration and control in high-pressure moments.

Regarding his salary, according to some estimates, Max Verstappen is the highest-paid driver in Formula 1, with an annual salary of €22 million.

101

Lewis Hamilton earned €35,000,000.

He is one of the most successful drivers in the history of Formula 1.

Born in Stevenage, England in 1985, Hamilton made his F1 debut in 2007 with the McLaren team and won the championship that same year.

Since then, he has won six more championships, becoming the second most successful driver in F1 history behind Michael Schumacher.

In 2013, Hamilton moved to the Mercedes team and has been a key part of their dominance in the hybrid era of F1.

He has achieved numerous victories and pole positions, and is known for his skill on wet tracks.

In addition to his on-track success, Hamilton has also been an active advocate for diversity and inclusion in the sport and has led the fight against racism in F1.

Outside of F1, Hamilton has also participated in fashion events and launched his own clothing line.

In 2021, Hamilton renewed his contract with Mercedes for one more year.

If you have enjoyed the curiosities about Formula 1 presented in this book, we would like to ask you to share a review on Amazon.

Your opinion is very valuable to us and to other Formula 1 enthusiasts who are looking to be entertained and learn new knowledge about this sport.

We understand that leaving a comment can be a tedious process, but we ask you to take a few minutes of your time to share your thoughts and opinions with us.

Your support is very important to us and helps us to continue creating quality content for fans of this incredible sport.

We appreciate your support and hope that you have enjoyed reading our book as much as we enjoyed writing it.

Thank you for sharing your experience with us!

★ ★ ★ ★ ★

Printed in Great Britain
by Amazon

34628760R00066